AF593784

WIT & WISDOM
FOR YOUR LIFE TOGETHER

Mike Yaconelli

To my wife Karla, whose gentle loving penetrated the walls of my soul and brought my heart back to life again.

Marriage is an adventure because our hearts know more than our minds.

Trust is not the
consequence of fidelity,
it is the result of listening
to each other.

Genuine love is full of surprises. That is why people who love each other always have a twinkle in their eye. The surprises never stop.

Before we were married we talked for hours and hours. Was I marrying my mother? Was she marrying her father? Absolutely not... we both agreed. Many years have passed now and sometimes when we are in bed for the evening and we say goodnight there is just a hint of a smirk on her lips as well as mine.

I know what she is thinking and she knows what I am thinking...

I married my mother. She married her father.

Faith is not the way out of
a troubled marriage,
it is the way *through* it.

A prayer

May these two people, now married, be a blessing and a comfort to each other, sharers of each other's joys, consolers in each other's sorrows, helpers to each other in whatever they set out to achieve. May they, trusting each other, trust life and not be afraid. May they continue to love each other forever.

My wife and I give each other an allowance. We can only spend the money on ourselves and we can spend it on anything we like. It is really fun and works great. Each of us can buy things we never would be able to justify if we took the money out of our monthly budget.

What makes sex great is not technique, but safety. Are we safe with each other in our nakedness and imperfection?

Love never gives up. Love cares more for others than for self. Love doesn't want what it doesn't have.

FROM THE FIRST LETTER TO THE CORINTHIANS,
THE MESSAGE

Love is more than words, but it *is* saying the words 'I love you'. Every day. Speaking them. Writing them. Singing them. Dancing them. Reading them. The words 'I love you' have a power all in themselves. The day you stop *saying* 'I love you' is the day your love starts to die.

As the years go by, the language of love adds to its vocabulary ... a touch, a squeeze, a wink, a turn of the head, a sigh, a twitch of the nose, a wrinkle of the mouth. If you are married long enough you can be together all day, never say a word, and yet carry on a lengthy conversation.

A good marriage is more than two people who love each other, it is two people who *like* each other.

… a man leaves father and mother and is firmly bonded to his wife, becoming one flesh – no longer two bodies but one. Because God created this organic union of the two sexes, no one should desecrate his art by cutting them apart.

FROM MATTHEW'S GOSPEL, *THE MESSAGE*

The Bible says that we are to leave our families and cleave to our spouse. Physically separating from our families is easy. Separating from the role we played in our family is much more difficult. Separating from the definition our family gave us is very difficult.

If our marriage is to survive, we not only leave home, we leave the family rules, the family definitions, the entire family system to create a new family.

Handwritten notes and letters to each other (and our children) is like giving a glimpse of our souls. Writing is the secret of intimacy. When we write we give our secrets permission to speak.

Enjoy life. This is not a dress rehearsal.

SUE MONK KIDD

What attracted you
to each other when you
were married are the same
things that will cause you
to divorce twenty years
later.

When you do what you always do, you get what you always get.

When couples stop laughing together love starts to die.

Romance is easy.
Loving is hard work.

A prayer

May our home truly be a
place of love and harmony
where your spirit
is ever present.

Sex in the movies is intimidating – it's either wild, uncontrolled passion characterized by the ripping of clothes, the smashing of furniture and the throwing of food, or it's sex of perfection with perfect bodies, perfect love-making and perfect orgasms.

The real sex of marriage is imperfect, inconsistent, and often interrupted by telephones, children and clocks. Good sex makes lousy movies and great marriages.

Every gift has a curse. You can't have one without the other. If your spouse is very organized, chances are they aren't too good at surprises. If you are impulsive, chances are you aren't too good at organization. That's *good*. That is why you were attracted to each other. Each of you needs what the other doesn't have.

No marriage can survive
without the words
'I'm sorry.'
No 'I'm sorry'
can survive without a
change of behaviour.

When you are in love there is power in the way your love says your name. Everyone calls me 'Mike'. My wife calls me 'Michael'. And when she says 'Michael' it is as though she has crawled deep into the crevices of my being and spoken the very essence of myself.

When she speaks my name, it is as though she has uncovered me ... *found* me. And I can whisper to those around me, 'She knows me. She *knows*.'

There is more to life than increasing its speed.

GHANDI

Love isn't made in bed, as though sex could manufacture what didn't already exist; rather, an existing love makes sex a lovely thing. Good sex won't save a marriage. Bad sex is seldom the primary cause of a marriage failure.

WALTER WANGERIN

When couples stop
laughing together, boredom
is just around the corner.

Instead of bickering over who will be at what home on Christmas and other days, we have created the 'Yaconelli National Holiday'. The dates are inviolate. Everyone in the family must attend our family weekend. No agenda. No gifts. Just a weekend together.

Fun is the fragrance
of love.

No marriage can survive without anger. Anger is the dark side of passion. Anger can be destructive, of course, but when it is constructive it dissolves the fear that hides our hurts.

Our life is so interesting that we have lost our taste for chit-chat. However, we are interested in everything, a pretty dress that goes by, a child with a mischievous smile, a kitten sleeping in a listless unconcerned fashion, what café has the best coffee. But a single word is enough to create closeness.

PAUL TOURNIER

Laziness is love's opposite.

M. SCOTT PECK,
THE ROAD LESS TRAVELLED

The success of your marriage is not determined by a set of principles that apply to everyone. The success of your marriage is determined by a unique set of principles that apply only to the two of you. It doesn't matter what works for everyone else, it matters what works for you. I do the cooking. She does the finances.

I do the shopping, she does the organizing. It doesn't matter whether or not it fits anyone else's mould, it fits ours.

Successful marriages are not clones of other successful marriages, they are a one-of-a-kind creation carved from a one-of-a-kind union of two one-of-a-kind people who have a one-of-a-kind love for each other.

Love is wanting to do what
you don't want to do
because you want to.

A prayer

Temper our hearts
with kindness,
oh God, there is
so little kindness.
May we not only
love each other,
but be kind
to each other.

I always know when a couple are in love. They are kind to each other.

Marriage has nothing to do with how many years you are together, it has to do with knowing.

Marriage is a daily expedition into the unknown territory of our spouse.

To be 'no longer two but one' is not only a question of participating in the same events and having sexual relations; it means to let our partner look deeply into our soul, to not have any secrets from the other.

PAUL TOURNIER

If I had my life to live over again, I would have invited friends over to dinner even if the carpet was stained and the sofa faded. I would have sat on the lawn with my children and not worried about grass stains. I would never have bought anything just because it was practical, wouldn't show soil or was guaranteed to last a lifetime.

When my child kissed me impetuously, I would never have said, ‘Later. Now get washed up for dinner.’ There would have been more ‘I love you’s, more ‘I’m sorry’s, but, mostly, given another shot at life, I would seize every minute, look at it and really see it, live it, and never give it back.

ERMA BOMBECK

Marriage is not about fixing, it's about *mixing*. Love doesn't drive us to fix the other person, it gives us the courage to *mix* strengths and weaknesses, our positives and negatives, our hopes and our fears into an invigorating marriage full of life and newness and dreams.

Loneliness is always a
symptom that love
is on holiday.

Love doesn't strut,
Doesn't have a swelled head,
Doesn't force itself on others,
Isn't always 'me first',
Doesn't fly off the handle,
Doesn't keep score of
the sins of others,
Doesn't revel when
others grovel,
Takes pleasure in the
flowering of truth,
Puts up with anything.

FROM THE FIRST LETTER TO THE CORINTHIANS,
THE MESSAGE

Tears are the words of
the soul and they must
always be listened to
because they tell us how
our love is doing.

One year we had no money for Christmas. We called a family meeting and decided to have a 'Coupon Christmas'. Each of us would give each other a booklet of coupons redeemable at any time. Coupons like 'I will wash the dishes when it's your turn.' 'Good for one car wash.'

My wife and I gave each child an 'anti-grounding certificate' (grounding is not being allowed to leave the house). Everyone in our family considers that Christmas the best we ever had.

Blessing

Father of all mankind,
make the roof of our house
wide enough for all opinions,
oil the door of our house so
that it opens easily to friend
and stranger and set such a
table in our house that the
whole family may speak kindly
and freely around it.

PRAYER FROM HAWAII (ADAPTED)

Love is like bread, it has to be made fresh every day.

AN OLD SAYING

Acknowledgments

Thanks go to those who have given permission to include material in this book, as indicated below. Every effort has been made to trace and contact copyright owners. If there are any inadvertent omissions or errors in the acknowledgments, we apologize to those concerned and will remedy them in the next edition.

Bible quotations reprinted from *The Message* are © 1993 Eugene Peterson. Used by permission of NavPress, Colorado Springs, CO. All rights reserved. For copies call (800) 366-7788.

Nelson Publishers for 'Love isn't made in bed' by Walter Wangerin, from *As for Me and my House*

HarperCollins US for 'Enjoy life' by Sue Monk Kidd from *When the Heart Waits*, and 'Laziness is love's opposite' by M. Scott Peck from *The Road Less Travelled*

Westminster/John Knox Press for 'To be no longer two but one' by Paul Tournier from *Secrets*

Published by
Lion Publishing plc
Sandy Lane West, Oxford, England
ISBN 0 7459 3445 5
Albatross Books Pty Ltd
PO Box 320, Sutherland, NSW 2232, Australia
ISBN 0 7324 1443 1

First edition 1996
10 9 8 7 6 5 4 3 2 1 0

A catalogue record for this book is available
from the British Library

Printed and bound in Singapore